Speed Machines

Dirt Bikes

By Matt Scheff

SportsZone
An Imprint of Abdo Publishing
www.abdopublishing.com

www.abdopublishing.com

Published by Abdo Publishing, a division of ABDO, PO Box 398166, Minneapolis, Minnesota 55439.

Printed in the United States of America, North Mankato, Minnesota
082014
012015

THIS BOOK CONTAINS RECYCLED MATERIALS

Cover Photo: Shutterstock Images
Interior Photos: Shutterstock Images, 1, 14-15, 26-27; Frank Mattia/NewSport/Corbis, 4-5; Hoppenworld.com/Jacob Kahn/AP Images, 6-7; Ernest King/AP Images, 8-9; Universal/TempSport/Corbis, 10-11; Dieter Demme/dpa/Corbis, 11; Pukhov Konstantin/Shutterstock Images, 12-13; Teemu Tretjakov/Shutterstock Images, 16-17; Gines Romero/Shutterstock Images, 18-19; Marcel Jancovic/Shutterstock Images, 20-21, 31; Ilya Andriyanov/Shutterstock Images, 22-23; Victor R. Caivano/AP Images, 24-25, 25; Eraldo Peres/AP Images, 28-29

Editor: Chrös McDougall
Series Designer: Nikki Farinella

Library of Congress Control Number: 2014944186

Cataloging-in-Publication Data
Scheff, Matt.
Dirt bikes / Matt Scheff.
p. cm. -- (Speed machines)
ISBN 978-1-62403-609-5 (lib. bdg.)
Includes bibliographical references and index.
1. Dirt bikes--Juvenile literature. 2. Trail bikes--Juvenile literature. I. Title.
629.227--dc23

2014944186

CONTENTS

PULLING AWAY

Fans get on their feet for the final of the 450 supercross event in Salt Lake City, Utah. Ryan Dungey is in the lead. But defending champion Ryan Villopoto is closing fast. Villopoto's green Kawasaki dirt bike sails over a jump and heads into a turn. He burns past Dungey into the lead.

Ryan Villopoto is one of the world's fastest dirt-bike racers.

Ryan Villopoto flies through the air during a supercross race.

FAST FACT

Villopoto won the American Motorcyclist Association supercross championship four straight years from 2011 to 2014.

With 10 laps to go, Dungey and Davi Millsaps are right on Villopoto's tail. Each rider challenges for the lead. But Villopoto holds them off. His tires dig into the dirt track, whipping around turns and speeding down straightaways. The crowd roars as he crosses the finish line in first place.

Motorcycles race off-road in 1938 in California.

THE HISTORY OF DIRT BIKES

The first motorcycles were built in the late 1800s. At the time, there were few paved roads. Most riders drove their motorcycles over dirt roads and across open land. That made these motorcycles the first dirt bikes. Paved roads soon became more common. Most motorcycles are now built for these paved roads. But some people prefer to ride off-road. By the early 1900s, people were holding cross-country motorcycle races called scrambles.

FAST FACT

One of the first motorcycles ever built was called "the boneshaker" because it gave such a rough and violent ride.

FAST FACT

Dirt bikes weren't just for sport. US soldiers rode dirt bikes on some missions during World War II in the 1940s.

A rider competes in a motocross race in the 1950s in France.

Dirt-bike racing exploded in popularity during the 1960s. The most popular event was motocross. Riders raced their custom-built racing bikes over jumps and around sharp curves. Fans loved it. Many wanted their own dirt bikes. Sales soared. Some people call this era the "Dirt Bike Boom."

Actor Steve McQueen, left, *prepares to go for a dirt-bike ride in 1964.*

A rider shows off a huge trick while going off a jump.

Dirt bikes continued to change over the next several decades. Engines got bigger and worked better. Meanwhile, dirt bike bodies got lighter and tougher. The top riders showed off their high-performance bikes in events ranging from motocross to cross-country races to freestyle trick competitions.

FAST FACT

Most early racing dirt bikes were built in Europe. But today, most high-performance dirt bikes come from Japan.

Dirt bikes are designed to handle rough terrain.

DIRT BIKE DESIGN

All dirt bikes share some basic features. The chassis is a strong, light metal frame. Everything else on the bike connects to the chassis. That includes the handlebars, body panels, tires, and fenders.

FAST FACT

Most dirt bikes are not allowed on US streets and highways. The bikes lack certain safety requirements, such as brake lights.

A suspension system connects the wheels to the chassis. This system of springs and shock absorbers allows the wheels to move over rough ground. It also provides a cushion when riders land from big jumps. Dirt bikes also need good grip on loose dirt and sand. So they have wide tires with deep tread.

A dirt bike drives through the mud.

A dirt bike powers through a motocross course.

FAST FACT

The fastest dirt bikes can go 125 miles per hour (201 km/h)—or faster!

A dirt bike's power depends on its engine size. A bigger engine produces more power. All dirt bike motors are measured in cubic centimeters (cc). Common sizes include 125cc, 250cc, and 450cc. Early dirt bikes all had two-stroke engines. They produced power by burning fuel with a series of two motions, or strokes. But modern racing bikes have four-stroke engines. The four-stroke engines are cleaner and more efficient.

PHOTO DIAGRAM

1. Helmet
2. Gloves
3. Chassis
4. Tire
5. Handlebars
6. Suspension system
7. Fender

1
2
5
7
6
4

Riders get ready to start a motocross race.

COMPETITION

Many people just ride dirt bikes for fun. But dirt bikes are also perfect for racing. Outdoor motocross races and indoor supercross races are among the most popular motor sports in the world. Riders speed around fixed courses, sail over jumps, rattle over bumps, and dig through sharp corners.

FAST FACT

The Dakar Rally started out as a race from Paris, France, to Dakar, Senegal. It moved to South America in 2009 due to security concerns.

A rider races down a sand dune in Chile during the 2014 Dakar Rally.

Longer cross-country races take place over natural terrain. Riders race over rocky mountains, sandy deserts, and hilly forests. The most famous cross-country race is the Dakar Rally. This race lasts several days. The 1992 edition was an amazing 7,722 miles (12,427 km).

The Dakar Rally travels through some remote areas.

FAST FACT

Enduro races have known checkpoints and secret checkpoints. The secret checkpoints help make sure the riders stay on the course.

Other riders take part in grueling enduro events. These riders must travel between a series of checkpoints over a long distance. Their goal is to pass each checkpoint at an exact set time. They get points for reaching a checkpoint too early or too late. The rider with the fewest points at the end is the winner.

A rider goes off-road in an enduro race.

Levi Sherwood performs a trick.

One of the most popular dirt bike competitions today is freestyle motocross (FMX). FMX riders take on huge jumps. They do tricks while their powerful dirt bikes soar through the air. Judges score each trick based on difficulty, style, originality, and landing.

FAST FACT

One of the hardest tricks in FMX is the double backflip. Motocross legend Travis Pastrana became the first rider to land this trick in 2006.

GLOSSARY

chassis
The main metal frame of a dirt bike.

enduro
A long dirt-bike competition in which riders are scored by how well they can reach checkpoints on time.

fender
A body panel that covers part of a vehicle, such as a wheel, to protect it from collisions.

motocross
A type of dirt-bike race usually held on large outdoor courses.

scramble
The name for the earliest cross-country dirt-bike races.

stroke
A movement of an engine's cylinders to burn fuel. Dirt bike engines can run on a series of two strokes or a series of four strokes.

supercross
A type of dirt-bike race held on small, tight courses in arenas or stadiums.

suspension system
The system of shock absorbers and springs that connects a dirt bike's chassis to its wheels.

terrain
The shape of natural land.

tread
A series of bumps and grooves that helps a tire grip a surface such as dirt or mud.

FOR MORE INFORMATION

Books
Mara, Wil. *Extreme Motocross*. New York: Marshall Cavendish, 2013.

Monnig, Alex. *Motocross Racing*. Minneapolis, MN: Abdo Publishing Co., 2014.

Websites
To learn more about Speed Machines, visit **booklinks.abdopublishing.com**. These links are routinely monitored and updated to provide the most current information available.

INDEX

ABOUT THE AUTHOR

Matt Scheff is a freelance author and lifelong motor sports fan living in Minnesota.